Jamaican Sayings

Life

Other titles in the series:

Jamaican Sayings
Character

Jamaican Sayings
Success

Andrea Campbell

I am grateful to my family

– Richmond and Shari –

for their love and support without which this book would not have been possible.

Jamaican Sayings

Life

Andrea M. Campbell, MBA MA

Publisher: AA Global Sourcing Ltd

Website: http://www.aaglobalsourcing.com

First Edition

First published in Great Britain in 2012 by

AA Global Sourcing Ltd

http://www.aaglobalsourcing.com

A catalogue record for this book is available from

The British Library

ISBN 978-1-4716-7941-4

Table of Contents

Introduction vii

Part 1

Sayings 1

Part II

Jamaica – An Insight 61

Jamaica – Land of Wood and Water ... 63

Map of Jamaica 67

National Symbols 68

Jamaica's National Heroes 71

Jamaican Anthem 74

National Song 75

National Pledge 75

National Prayer 76

Shorter Pledge for Schools 77

Governors General 79

Prime Ministers 81

Out of Many, One People 83

Glossary 89

Introduction

Jamaican Sayings - Life is the first in a series of three books that capture Jamaican adages used to communicate ideas about human nature, behaviour, relationships, aspirations, health, hope and survival. *Jamaican Sayings - Character* and *Jamaican Sayings - Success* complete the series.

The adages represent an archive of the wit and wisdom of many generations and aim to trigger reflection and thought. In their use they are never fully explained but those to whom they are directed usually understand their meaning based on the context in which they are used. They utilise imagery and draw upon a variety of flora and fauna to enrich their content. They hold valuable lessons, inspiration and wisdom that link Jamaican culture to its African past.

The sayings are presented in three parts:

i) the original saying;
ii) the literal English translation and
iii) the meaning it aims to convey.

As shown in the table of contents, the second part of Jamaican Sayings – Life includes valuable information on Jamaica's history, national symbols and leaders.

On the cover:

Ackees (Jamaican National Fruit)
Lignum Vitae (Jamaican National Flower)
Banana plant
Coffee plant
Blue Mahoe (Jamaican National Tree)

1. Ackee lub fat, ocra lub salt

Ackee loves fat, okra loves salt

i) People will pursue whatever they deem attractive;
ii) Everyone has his own taste.

2. Ah noh ebery day ah Krismus

Not every day is Christmas

You will not always get what you want.

3. Ah noh ebery shut yeye ah sleep

It is not every time that you shut your eyes that you are sleeping

Appearances are not always what they seem.

4. **Ah noh ebery mango gat maggige**

It is not every mango that has maggots

Everyone is not the same; people have different characteristics and you shouldn't make assumptions or generalise.

5. **Ah noh one day monkey waah wife**

It's not for just on one day only that a monkey wants sexual favours

It's not just once that you will want a favour; show some gratitude to those who support you!

6. **Ah noh want ah fat mek nightingale foot tan so**

It's not for the lack of fat why a nightingale's feet are like that

You shouldn't judge by appearances (Don't judge a book by its cover).

7. All duck noh dabble inna one hole

All ducks do not dabble in the same hole

Be mindful of the fact that people belong to different social classes.

8. All kine ah fish eat man, only shaak get blame

All types of fish eat people but only sharks are blamed for it

If you have a bad reputation you will be blamed for everything, even when you are innocent.

9. Alligetta lay egg, but im noh fowl

Alligators lay eggs but alligators are not fowls

People may engage in similar activities but that does not mean that they are alike.

10. Ants fallaw fat, bees fallaw honey

Ants follow fat, bees follow honey

People naturally gravitate to prosperity and affluence.

11. Anyting inna dark mus com ah lite

Anything in the dark must come to light

Anything that is done in the dark will be revealed in due course.

12. Anyting tan too lang serve two master

Anything that stays too long will serve two masters

If you don't make use of what you have, someone else will.

13. Anyway ih mawga ih pap

Anywhere it becomes thin it will break

There's no point in worrying about scarce resources - make the best use of what you have.

14. Bad fambily betta dan empty pigsty

A bad family is better than an empty pigsty

Family is important and no matter how bad you think they are, you should treasure them!

15. Bad luck woss dan obeah

Bad luck is worse than obeah

We all need some luck in life.

16. Beetle nebber right befoe hen

A beetle is never right in the sight of a hen

Your enemies will always judge you harshly.

17. Befoe dawg go widout supper, im nyam cackroach

To avoid going without supper, a dog will eat cockroaches

People will resort to unconventional measures when circumstances dictate the need.
Desperate situations call for desperate measures
(Any port in a storm)

18. Betta fish inna di sea dan wats already caught

There is better fish is in the sea than those that are already caught

There are always other and perhaps better choices available. (There is no need to rush.)

19. Blood ticka dan wahta

Blood is thicker than water

Family comes first; irrespective of what your family may do to you, they have priority – at the end of the day, they are your family.

20. Bud sing sweet fi im owna nes

Birds sing sweetly for their own nests

People save the best for themselves.

21. Buy meat yuh get bone, buy lan yuh get stoane

If you buy meat, you get bones; if you buy land you get stones

There is no perfection in life; there are weaknesses all around; make the best of what you've got.

22. Brown man wife nyam cackroach ah cawna, sabe money fi buy silk dress

A brown man's wife eats cockroaches in the corner while she saves her money to buy silk dresses

Some people disguise the fact that they are poor by pretending to be rich.

23. Cat noh mek no dawg

Cats do not produce dogs

Children are likely to follow in their parents' footsteps; You'll reap the harvest of whatever seeds you sow.

24. Chair fall dung bench get up

The chair falls down the bench gets up

No one is indispensable;
One man's loss is another man's gain.

25. Chicken merry, hawk deh near

A chicken may be merry but a hawk is nearby

You should always be careful, even when you are having fun.

26. Chip nebber fly far fram di black

A chip never falls far from the block

i) People of the same family or background have similar traits;
ii) It is natural for children to emulate their parents.

27. Cowad man keep soun bone

A coward man keeps sound bones

While it may be acceptable to be adventurous and take risks, be aware that risk-taking is dangerous and you could get hurt.

28. Cow nebba know di use ah im tail till im lose ih

A cow doesn't know the use of its tail until it loses it

You don't appreciate who or what you have until you no longer have them;
Take nothing or no-one for granted.

29. Cow noh dead im wi shake im tail

A cow that is not dead will shake its tail

Never give up on someone while they are still alive.
(While there's life there's hope)

30. Cow seh "Tan up noh mean res"

Cow says, "Standing up does not mean resting"

Appearances can be deceiving.

31. Crab cyaan hol inna lobster shell

A crab cannot fit into a lobster's shell

Be aware of social barriers; know your place.

32. Crab seh im noh trus noh shedda afta dawk

The crab says that he doesn't trust any shadow after dark

You have a right to be sceptical when dealing with people who are shady in their dealings.

33. Cry-cry boot noh good fi aise

A squeaking boot is no good for the ears

No one enjoys hearing constant complaints.

34. Cuss-cuss noh bore ole inna mi kin

Curses bore no hole in my skin

Mere words cannot inflict physical pain.

35. Cuss Jankro peel ed an turkey bex

If you curse a crow about its bald-head a turkey will be vexed

If you offend someone, you also offend his kind and they too become your enemies.

36. Cyaan tan fur trow salt inna pat

You cannot stay far and throw salt in a pot

Don't share sensitive information from a distance; be discreet!

37. Dawg cyaan manage bone im throw ih weh, fowl go pick ih up

When a dog cannot manage a bone it throws it away, yet a fowl goes and picks it up

If the experts cannot handle a situation, don't assume you can!

38. Dawg foot bruk im fine im massa yard

A dog's foot is broken he finds his master's yard

i) Those who get hurt in life will find their way back home;
ii) Things happen to us in life that make us return to our roots.

39. Dawg nebber fight ova dry bone

Dogs never fight over dry bones

i) If you are fighting over an issue, make sure it's worth fighting for;
ii) Don't waste your time on someone or something that won't add value to you.

40. Dawg seh if im av money im wouda buy im owna fleas

A dog said that if it had money it would buy its own fleas

When some people have money they waste it on unnecessary things.

41. Deble ole but im noh bedridden

The devil is old but not bedridden

People who are wicked when they are young don't change simply because they have grown older.

42. Dere's no disease dat time cyaan cure

There is no disease that time cannot cure

Time is the master; everything will fall into place in due course.

43. Di moe yuh lib di moe yuh larn

The longer you live the more you learn

Wisdom increases with age;
Learning is a lifelong activity

44. Di olda de bull di stiffer di horn

The older the bull, the stiffer the horns

The older you get the more assertive (and perhaps more stubborn) you become;
Old habits are hard to change

45. Di olda di clock di fassser ih wine

The older the clock the faster it winds

People become wiser as they grow older.

46. Di olda di moon di bryta ih shine

The older the moon, the brighter it shines

Wisdom increases with age.

47. **Di only cure fi sleep ah sleep**

The only cure for sleep is sleep

Irrespective of how busy you are you must find time to sleep (and rest).

48. **Duck an fowl feed togeda but dem noh roos togeda**

Ducks and chickens may feed together but they do not dwell together

People from different social classes may interact out of necessity but don't expect this interaction to go beyond a certain level.

49. Duppy know who fi frighten

Ghosts know whom they should frighten

i) Bullies know who to pick on;
ii) People will always heckle those they perceive to be weaker.

50. Ebery danki sing fram im own hymn sheet

Every donkey sings from his own hymn sheet

Every man to his own order;
People protect their own interest.

51. Ebery day yuh ah beat donkey one day im ah go kick yuh

If every day you beat a donkey one day it will kick you

People have a limit as to how much abuse they will tolerate before they retaliate.

52. Ebery fambily av im bruk foot

Every family has its own broken leg

Every family has vulnerable members.

53. Ebery oe av im tick ah bush

Every hoe has its matching stick in the bush

There is someone for everyone.

54. Ebery tinking fish hab im buyer

Every stinking fish has its buyer

There is someone for everyone.

55. Ebery tun yuh tun macca juk yuh

Every time you turn thorns prick your skin

Trials and tribulations abound in life.

56. Eye lash olda dan beard

The eyelash is older than the beard

Show respect to your elders.

57. Eye noh si haart noh leap

What the eyes don't see doesn't affect the heartbeat

What you don't know doesn't hurt you.

58. Fire deh ah muss-muss tail, im tink ah cool breeze

Fire is at a mouse' tail it thinks it's cool breeze

You may be heading for trouble and not even realise it.

59. Fish ah deep water noh know ow fish ah rivvaside feel

Fish in deep waters don't know how the fish in shallow waters feel

i) People who live in a secure environment cannot understand how those who live in dangerous situations feel;
ii) Rich people don't understand the suffering of the poor.

60. Fish-bone noh ladge inna pickney troat alone

Fish bones don't lodge in children's throats only

Misfortune takes no account of age or vulnerability; it strikes anyone.

61. Fowl feed ah han eezy fi ketch

A chicken that's fed by hand is easily caught

Those close to us are easily caught.

62. Hog seh why yuh mout so lang, mumma seh you ah com you wi si

Hog asked: why is your mouth so long?
The mother answered: you are coming, you will see

Though you fail to understand some key lessons when you are young, in time all becomes clear.

63. Hungry belly an full belly noh walk ah pass

A hungry belly and a full belly don't share the same path

Those with money cannot comprehend the misery of those without.

64. If ah noh soh ah neally soh

If it's not like that, it is nearly that

There is often some truth in stories you hear on the grapevine.

65. If fool noh go ah market bad sinting noh sell

If fools don't go to market, foolishness won't sell well.

Don't complain about the bad purchases you made; spend your money wisely!

66. Ih haad fi get butta outta dawg troat

It is difficult to take butter out of a dog's throat

It is hard to get anything from miserly people.

67. If yuh barn fi heng yuh cyaan drown

If you are born to be hanged you cannot drown

Every man has his own destiny.

68. If yuh crape gourdy yuh fine worm-ole

If you scrape a gourdy you will find worm holes

If you search for faults you will find them.

69. If yuh noh done nyam noh dash weh yuh plate

If you haven't finished eating, don't discard your plate

Don't celebrate prematurely; it is not over until it is truly over.

70. If you waah fi know if mawga dawg av teeth draw im tail

If you want to know if a meagre dog has teeth, tug at its tail

Don't be tempted to interfere with peaceful people or you will be surprised by their wrath.

71. If yuh waah half a bread beg smaddy buy ih but if yuh waah wan buy ih yuself

If you want half of a loaf, ask someone to buy it but if you want a complete bread go and buy it yourself

If you want something done properly, do it yourself.

72. In de lang run di cheapes ah di deares

In the long run the cheapest is the dearest

What appears to be the cheapest can cost considerably more in the long term.

73. In ebery poun ah lie dere is a ounce ah truth

In every pound of lie there is an ounce of truth

i) There is usually some degree of truth, however minute, in gossip;
ii) If you examine a negative situation closely, you will find something positive

74. Jankro seh im cyaan wok pon Sunday

Crow says that he cannot work on Sundays

People cannot be forced to work on public holidays if they really don't want to do so.

75. Jump outta frying pan an inna di fire

Jump out of frying pan and into the fire

Be careful that you are not leaving a bad situation for a similar or worse one.

76. Kick dawg im fren yuh, feed im im bite yuh

If you kick a dog he will befriend you but if you feed him, he will bite you

Some people respond better to bad treatment.

77. Kiss ass befoe yuh lick ih

Kiss an arse before you slap it

In order to appeal to someone, you need to be humble but once you have what you want you no longer have to grovel.

78. Kunnu no hab good bottam im cyaan go ah sea

If a canoe does not have a good bottom it cannot go to the sea

People must ensure that their foundation is sound before they build on it.

79. Lawya look pan yuh wid one yeye but im look pan yuh packet wid two

A lawyer looks at you with one eye but uses both eyes to inspect your pocket

Some people have no time for you but will find the time if they feel that they can benefit financially.

80. Lass pickney kill mumma

The last child kills his mother

There is a limit to everything – the last straw breaks the camel's back.

81. Likkle bit ah ram goat ave beard an big bull noh av nun

A little ram goat may have a beard whereas a big bull has none

Younger people or those smaller in stature often have great attributes that are lacking in more mature people or those of a larger frame.

82. Likkle bud cyaa seeds very far

Little birds carry seeds very far

Be careful what you say in the presence of little children, they are good at bearing tales.

83. Likkle wabba av big aise

Little warblers have big ears

Be careful what you say in the presence of children.

***84.* Lizard nebber know weh im deh till im fine himself inna puss mout**

A lizard never knows where he is until he finds himself in a cat's mouth

People often realise that they are in trouble only when it's too late.

***85.* Lizard noh fraid fi walk ah road late because im noh good fi nyam**

Lizards are not edible so they are not afraid to walk on the streets late at night

People with nothing to lose will take more risks.

***86.* Lang road draw sweat short cut draw blood**

Long road draws sweat short cut draws blood

The shortest route is not always the best one; Although the longer route can be tiring, it is often the better choice.

***87.* Man ah sea noh know how man ah lan feel**

A man at sea doesn't know how a man ashore feels

Wealthy people do not truly comprehend the suffering of the poor.

88. Man hab cow im look fi milk

A man with cow looks for milk

People base their expectations on their personal circumstances.

89. Man dat carry straw noh fi fool wid fire

Someone who carries straw shouldn't play with fire

Those who are vulnerable in certain situations should exercise caution. (If you live in a glass house, don't throw stones)

90. Man av raw meat im look fi fire

A man who has raw meat looks for a fire

If you have problems, proactively look for solutions; don't expect them to be sorted by someone else.

91. Man nebber know de use ah water till di tank run dry

A man never knows the use of water until the tank runs dry

People often do not appreciate others until they no longer have access to them.

92. Man noh dead noh call im duppy

If a man is not dead, don't call him a ghost

As long as someone is alive, don't dismiss their potential; don't write them off.

93. Man no pread clothes ah doah im noh watch rain

If a man has not spread out his clothes to dry he does not watch the rain

If you have nothing to lose you won't be unduly concerned about threats.

94. Man widout wife like a kitchen widout a knife

A man without a wife is like a kitchen without a knife

People need companionship.

95. Mangoose seh man who cyaan tek risk ah noh man at all

The mongoose says that a man who can't take risks is not a man

Risk-taking is a life skill; it promotes maturity.

96. Many ways to heng a dawg without putting rope roun im neck

There are many ways to hang a dog without putting a rope around its neck

There are many strategies that can be used to get even with someone.

97. Mek a fren when yuh noh need one

Make friends even when you don't need them

Don't wait until you need favours from people before you seek to build relationships with them.

98. Mischief com by di poun an go by di ounce

Mischief comes in pounds but leaves in ounces

Getting into trouble is easy but getting out of it is far more difficult.

99. Monkey si monkey do

What a monkey sees it will copy

People are social beings that enjoy copying the actions of others.

100. Naizy rivva noh drown nobady

A noisy river doesn't drown anyone

Argumentative people are harmless in reality.

101. Noh all foot inna boot ah good foot

Not all feet in boots are good feet

Appearances can be deceiving.

102. Noh ax hungry duck fi watch kaan

Don't ask a hungry duck to watch corn

Don't put temptations in people's way.

103. Noh buy cow if yuh can get free milk

There is no need to buy a cow if you can obtain milk free of charge

Why pay for something if you can have it free of cost.

104. Noh buy puss inna bag

Don't buy a cat in a bag

Sample your goods before you buy them.

105. Noh gi rat cheese fi carry

Don't give a rat cheese to carry

Don't put temptation in the way of needy or greedy people.

106. Noh swap black dawg fi monkey

Don't swap a black dog for a monkey

Be careful not to exchange one bad situation for another.

107. Nuff bone ah dungle come fram good man table

Many bones in the dung heap came from good men's tables

Many seemingly worthless people come from good families.

***108.* Ole ooman ah swear fi nyam callalu, callalu ah swear fi wok ol ooman belly**

An old woman is swearing for callaloo while the callaloo is swearing for the old woman

You may be planning for someone but be warned, they may be planning for you too.

109. Ole ooman half ah hoe bring new one

An old woman's half a hoe brings a new one

Be careful when using other people's faulty items as you may have to replace them.

110. Old fiah-tick easy fi lite

An old fire-stick is easy to light

An old flame (former lover) can easily re-enter your life.

111. Once bitten twice shy

If you are bitten once you will be shy the next time

If you have been adversely affected by a particular situation, you will exercise caution in future.

112. One hand cyaan clap

One hand cannot clap

We need to support each other; it is difficult for people to be successful without some amount of assistance.

113. Only shoe know ef stockin hab ole

Only shoes know if there is a hole in the stocking

Only those who are close enough to you know your weaknesses.

114. Orange yellah but yuh noh know ef ih sweet

The orange is yellow but you don't know if it's sweet

Don't judge by appearances.
(Don't judge a book by its cover)

115. Parson cyaan preach wid dutty collar cause all yeye deh pon im

A pastor cannot preach with a dirty collar because all eyes are on him

If you are in a position of moral authority,
you must lead by example.

116. Parson christen im pickney fus

A pastor christens his child first

People look after their own interests first.

117. Pickney suck dem mumma wen dem young an dem puppa wen dem ole

Children suck their mothers when they are young and their fathers when they get older

Children rely on their mothers when they are young but are a drain on their father's resources as they grow older.

118. Platn ripe cyaan green agaen

Once a plantain is ripe it cannot go
Back to green

Once innocence is lost it can never be regained.

119. Poah man pickney walk one-one, rich man pickney walk gang-gang

A poor man's child walks alone while a
rich man's child is well accompanied

Those with money have many friends while for those without it is a lonely road.

120. Man poah im wod poah

If a man is poor his word is poor

Those without money are powerless.

121. Pot ah cuss kettle seh im battam black

A pot is cursing a kettle by saying its
Bottom is black

There is no point in being unkind to someone who has vulnerabilities similar to yours.

122. Puss belly full rat batty tink

When a cat's belly is full, a rat's
bottom is stink

When people don't want something they are prone to finding faults (which are often non-existent).

123. Puss gone rat tek charge

When the cat's away, the mouse takes over

When those in authority are absent, those left behind will do as they please.
(When the cat's away the mice will play)

124. Puss an dawg noh av di same luck!

A cat and a dog do not have the same luck

i) Favouritism will change outcomes;
ii) What works for some people will not work for others.

125. Rain ah fall but dutty tough

It is raining but the dirt is still tough

Some people live in extreme poverty while there is prosperity all around.

126. Rain noh fall ah one man door

It doesn't rain at one man's door only

No one has all the luck.

127. Rat belly full potato av kin

When a rat's belly is full,
potato has skin

When you're not in need, you can afford to be unduly selective.

128. Sarry fi poah ting, poah ting kill yuh

Sorry for Poor Thing, Poor Thing kills you

Sometimes you help someone and they hurt you in return.

129. Sensé fowl noh waah fedder but im waah carn

Sensé fowl doesn't want feathers,
It wants corn

i) Don't assume you know what is good for other people;
ii) Appearances cannot always be interpreted literally.

130. Snake weh waah fi grow up stay inna im ole

A snake that wants to grow up remains in its hole

People should stay within their social circles until they have learnt key lessons of life in order to cope in the wider society.

131. Stoane ah rivva battam noh know sun hat

A stone at the bottom of a river doesn't know the heat of the sun

If you are always sheltered and protected it will be difficult for you to comprehend the concept of hardship.

132. Stranja noh walk ah back door

Strangers do not walk at the back door

Only your friends can hurt you; your enemies cannot get near enough.

133. Those who cyaan dance seh di music noh good

Those who don't know how to dance say the music is no good

People will find faults and make excuses if they find that they are unable to cope in a situation.

134. Tom drunk but Tom noh fool

Tom may be drunk but Tom is no fool

Appearances can be deceiving.

135. Trubble mek big man wear pickney shut

When in trouble a grown man will wear a child's shirt

When in trouble people will take unconventional and creative actions to get out.

136. Trubble mek puss run up prickly pear

Trouble makes a cat run
up a prickly pear plant

When people are in trouble they are more likely to take risks.

137. Trubble noh set like rain

Trouble doesn't announce its coming
like the rain does

You don't always see trouble looming; it often just happens; be careful!

138. Wall hab aise

Walls have ears

Be aware of your surroundings, you don't know who may be listening.

139. Wah ah fun fi bwoy ah det fi bullfrag

What is fun to a boy is death to a frog

What one person finds funny the other person finds painful.

140. Wah noh cost nutten gib good meja

What costs nothing gives good measure

People tend to be generous with items that are of no cost to them.

141. Wah drop offa head drop pon shoulder

What drops from the head falls onto the shoulder

i) He who makes the effort often does not reap the rewards;
ii) Sometimes an item that was meant for you is given instead to members of your family.

142. Wah noh happn inna year happen inna day

What doesn't happen in a year happens in a day

A long awaited event can happen suddenly; There isn't always a precursor to an occurrence. (It's never too late for a shower of rain)

143. Wah sweet nanny goat ah go run im belly

What is sweet to a nanny goat now will later give him diarrhoea

The things that seem enjoyable to you in one moment can hurt you later.

144. Wah sweet yuh gwine sour yuh

What is sweet to you will become sour

The source of your enjoyment now could cause you pain later.

145. Wat yuh doan know olda dan yuh

What you don't know is older than you

Knowledge comes with age and experience.

146. Wah gone bad ah morning, cyaan come good ah evenin

What's gone bad in the morning cannot be good in the evening

If a situation starts badly, it will end badly.

147. Wen a lian sleep doan wake im

When a lion is asleep, don't wake him

When a bad situation has been put to rest, don't revisit it unnecessarily.

148. When bull get ole yuh tek plantain trash fi tie him

When a bull gets old you can use plantain trash to tie him

People who were once powerful are subject to ridicule when they lose their power.

149. When bull ole im feed ah fence side

When a bull is old it feeds at the side of the fence

Caution increases with age.

150. Wen chicken tie up cackroach waan explanation

When a chicken is tied up the cockroach wants an explanation

When your enemies appear too feeble, friendly or harmless, that's cause for suspicion; be careful.

151. Wen cackroach get inna trubble im well glad fi run go hide ah fowl-house

When a cockroach gets into trouble it is happy to hide in a hen house

People implement any available solution when they find themselves in trouble.
(Any port in a storm)

152. Wen cackroach av party im noh ax fowl

When a cockroach throws a party he doesn't invite fowls

It's unwise to invite your enemies to dine with you.

153. Wen crab walk to much im luze im claw

When a crab walks too much it loses its claw

If you overuse an item it will eventually be rendered useless.

154. Wen fiah an water mek fren anybody can lib

When fire and water become friends people can live

When mortal enemies bury the hatchet peace will reign.

155. Wen snake bite yuh, yuh si lizzard yuh run

When you have been bitten by a snake you run from a lizard

Painful experiences cause people to become overly cautious.

156. Wen trubble tek yuh pickney shut fit yuh

When trouble takes you a child's shirt will fit you

When you are in trouble, you accept any help available. (A drowning man holds on to a straw)

157. Wen two dawg fight over bone annoda dawg run weh wid ih

Two dogs fight over a single bone; another dog comes and takes it away

Ardent contenders often lose the prize to someone else.

158. Wen visita come ah wi fireside wi mek wi pot smell nice

When visitors come to our fireside, we ensure that our pot smells nice

Be hospitable to your guests and exhibit good manners in their presence.

159. Wen yellow snake ded yuh can meja im

When a (poisonous) yellow snake dies, you can measure him

The dead has no power over the living.

160. Wen yuh cyaan fight bushman yuh tek weh im bush

If you are unable to fight a bushman just take away his bush

If you are unable to overcome your enemy remove his protection or power source.

161. Wen yuh get fambily bikkle nyam ih; when yuh hea fambily row, run!

When your family offers you food, accept it but when you hear family disputes, run!

Eat and drink with your family but do all you can to avoid getting involved into family disputes.

162. Wah fit masquita cyaan fit elephant

What fits a mosquito cannot fit an elephant

Not every style or situation will suit everyone. (Different strokes for different folks)

163. Who God bless no man curse

He who God blesses,
no man can curse

If God has blessed you, no one can hurt you.

164. Yuh nebber see kickin cow widout kickin calf

You will never a see a kicking cow without
a kicking calf

Children imitate their parents.

165. Yuh nebber si pop-gun kill alligetta

One cannot use a pop-gun to kill an
alligator

Don’t send a boy to do a man's job.

166. Yuh nebber si smoke widout fiah

Where there's smoke there's fire

Suspicions and rumours are often based on facts.

167. Young bud noh know bout storm

A young bird doesn't know about storms

Young people lack life experience and are prone to making decisions that may be to their detriment.

168. Young bud noh know haard time

A young bird doesn't know hard times

Young people do not understand the challenges of life.

169. Young bud noh know wen berry ripe ah mounten

A young bird doesn't know when there are ripe berries in the mountain

There is much to learn from the experience and knowledge of older people.

170. Yuh bes fren ah yuh woss enemy

Your best friend is your worst enemy

Those who are closest to you are in a position to hurt you the most.

171. Yuh can tek de hawse to the wahta but yuh cyaan mek im drink ih

You can take the horse to the water but you can't make it drink

You cannot make an individual do something that they really don't want to do.

172. Yuh cyaan tan blow no play wid tick

If you can't take blows, don't play with sticks

Don't venture into areas where you cannot handle all the possible consequences.

173. Yuh gi dawg food inna plate im tek ih out put pan grung

When you feed a dog in a plate it takes out the food and places it on the ground

Some people aren't accustomed to quality so there is no point forcing it onto them.

174. Yuh know weh yuh barn but yuh noh know weh you ah go bury

You know where you were born but you don't know where you will be buried

The past is known, the future is uncertain.

175. Yuh life lang but yuh cayliss wid ih

Your life is long but you are careless with it

Careless people take unnecessary risks.

176. Yuh nebber know de use ah yuh battam till boil bruk out

You never know the use of your bottom until a boil breaks out

You don't appreciate the usefulness of something until you no longer have it.

177. Yuh pickney ah go bite yuh aise

Your child is going to bite your ears

If you don't discipline your child you will live to regret it.

178. Yuh shake man han yuh noh shake im heart

You can shake a man's hand but not his heart

You can never know for sure what someone is thinking;
Open expressions are not necessarily true reflections of the heart.

179. Yuh si hous tan up, yuh noh go inside, yuh noh know ow ih tan

You don't know the true state of a house until you enter

Until you get to the bottom of a story it is unwise to draw a conclusion.

Part II

Jamaica – An Insight

Jamaica – Land of Wood and Water

Jamaica is a beautiful place and Jamaicans are an amazing people. We are well known for our beaches, delicious food and Reggae music, but as a people we have progressed way beyond the obvious and have excelled and impacted in almost every sphere of life. Here we present a taste of Jamaica – a few of the people who have made contributions, national symbols, customs, fauna and flora.

Communication – Jamaica has a fully digital telephone communication system (landline, internet, mobile and entertainment)

Culture – Jamaica is rich in culture and has a strong global presence. The musical genres reggae, ska, mento, rocksteady, dub, and, more recently, dancehall and ragga all originated on the island.

Currency – Jamaica's currency is the Jamaican dollar. Bank notes are issued for the following amounts: J$50, J$100, J$500, J$1000 and J$5000.

Economy – Jamaica is a mixed economy with both state enterprises and private sector businesses. Major sectors of the Jamaican economy include agriculture, mining, manufacturing, tourism, and financial and insurance services.

Geography – Jamaica is the third largest Caribbean island, measuring 145 miles (234 km) at its widest point. The climate in Jamaica is tropical, with hot and humid weather, although higher inland regions are more temperate. There is no definite rainy season but it rains mostly in May and October.

Government and Politics – Jamaica is an independent state with an elected Parliament, a Prime Minister, an elected House of Representatives and a Senate. The head of state is Queen Elizabeth II and her representative on the island is the Governor General. Jamaica is a member of the Commonwealth of Nations.

Education – Education is free from the early childhood to secondary levels.

History – Arawak and Taino indigenous people originating from South America settled on the island between 4000 and 1000 BC. Columbus arrived in 1494 and claimed Jamaica for Spain. The Spanish were defeated by the British in 1655 and the country achieved independence from Britain on 6 August 1962.

Industries – tourism, bauxite, agriculture (sugar, bananas, coffee, pimento, cocoa and tobacco).

Language – The official language of Jamaica is English. Jamaicans also speak Jamaican Patois, which has become known widely through the spread of Reggae music.

Population – Just under 3,000,000 people from the following ethnic groups: African, Indian, Chinese, Lebanese, Syrian, English, Scottish, Irish, and German.

Religion – Christians make up the majority of the population. Other popular religions in Jamaica include Islam, Bahá'í Faith, Buddhism, and Hinduism and Jews.

Sports – Cricket, athletics and football are popular; other sports include boxing, horseracing, golf, netball, volleyball, chess, basketball and dominoes.

Transport – Road, rail, sea and air transport, with roadways forming the backbone of the island's internal transport system.

Map of Jamaica

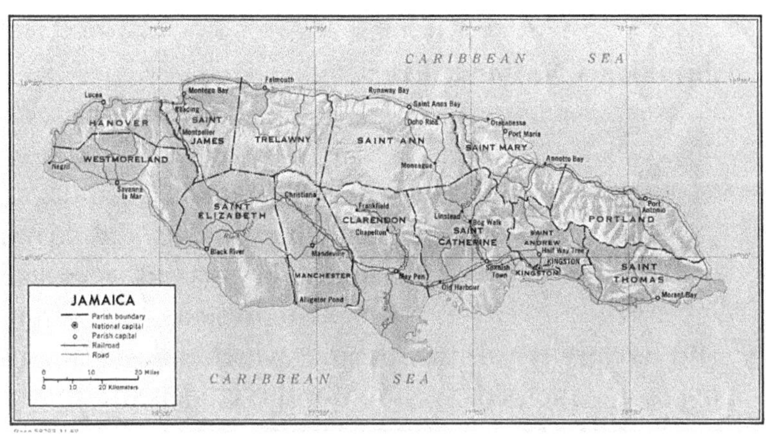

Our Neighbours

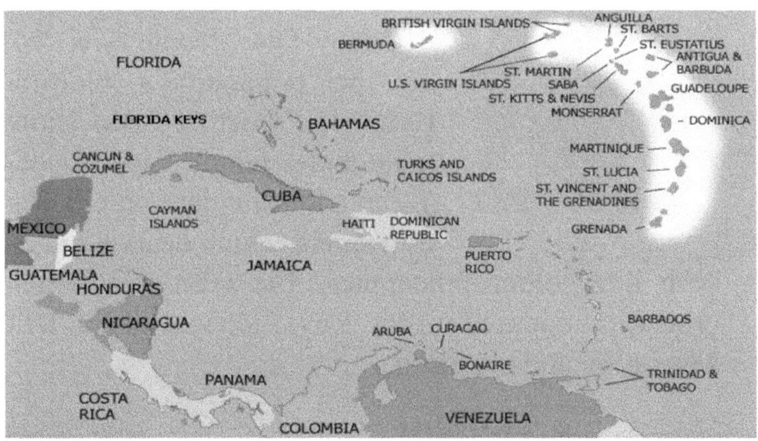

National Symbols

Jamaica's National Flag

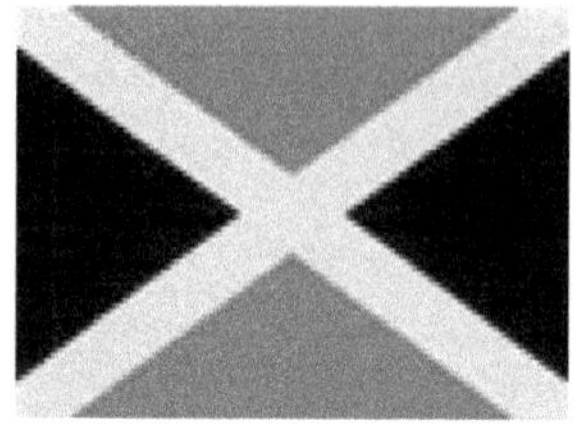

The Flag was first raised on Independence Day - 6 August 1962. It depicts memories of past achievements and provides inspiration for further success. Black represents the strength and creativity of the people which allows them to overcome the odds, yellow for the golden sunshine and green for the lush vegetation of the island.

The Jamaican Coat of Arms

The Jamaican national motto - Out of Many One People – is based on the population's multiracial roots. The Coat of Arms shows a male and a female member of the Taino tribe standing on either side of a shield which bears a red cross with five golden pineapples. The crest is a Jamaican crocodile mounted on the Royal Helmet of the British Monarchy and mantling.

The National Flower – Lignum Vitae

(Guiacum officinale)

The Lignum Vitae (wood of life) has medicinal qualities. The plant is extremely ornamental, producing an attractive blue flower and orange-yellow fruit. The tree is one of the most useful in the world. The body, gum, bark, fruit, leaves and blossom all serve some useful purpose.

The National Bird - The Doctor Bird

(Trochilus polytmus)

The doctor bird or swallow tail humming bird is found only in Jamaica. Its beautiful feathers have no counterpart in the entire bird population and they produce iridescent colours characteristic only of that family. The mature male has two long tails which stream behind him when he flies.

The National Tree – The Blue Mahoe

(Hibiscus Elatus)

The Blue Mahoe is indigenous to the island and grows quite rapidly. It has a straight trunk, broad green leaves and hibiscus-like flowers which change colour from bright yellow to orange red and finally to crimson. The Blue Mahoe is used for timber, making furniture and for making decorative objects. Cuba is the only other place where the Blue Mahoe grows naturally.

The National Fruit – The Ackee (Blighia sapida)

Originally imported to the island from West Africa, Ackee is derived from the original name Ankye which comes from the Twi language of Ghana. There are two main types of ackees - soft yellow 'butter' ackee and hard, cream-coloured 'cheese' ackee. The fruit contains a poison (hypoglcin) which is dissipated when it is properly harvested and cooked.

The National Dish – Ackee and Saltfish

Tasty dish made with ackee, codfish, tomatoes, peppers onions, black pepper and pimento. Serve with fried or boiled dumplings, roast breadfruit, hard dough bread or boiled green bananas.

Jamaica's National Heroes

Sir Alexander Bustamante (1884-1977)
A charismatic and impressive speaker and leader who understood the dynamics of labour relations. The years 1937 and 1938 brought the outbreak of widespread discontent and social unrest and Bustamante became the champion of the working class. In 1943 he founded the Jamaica Labour Party (JLP), and in 1962 became the first Prime Minister of Independent Jamaica.

Norman Washington Manley (1893-1969)
A brilliant scholar, athlete, soldier and lawyer, Manley identified with the cause of the workers at the time of the labour troubles of 1938 and in September of that year founded the People's National Party (PNP). He was elected PNP President annually until he retired in 1969.
Manley's and Bustamante's efforts resulted in the New Constitution of 1944 granting full Adult Suffrage.

Marcus Mosiah Garvey (1887-1940)
Garvey sought the unification of all Blacks through the establishment of the United Negro Improvement Association (UNIA) which he started in 1914 and he spoke out against economic exploitation and cultural denigration. The UNIA, which grew into an international organisation, encouraged self-government for black people worldwide; self-help economic projects and protest against racial discrimination.

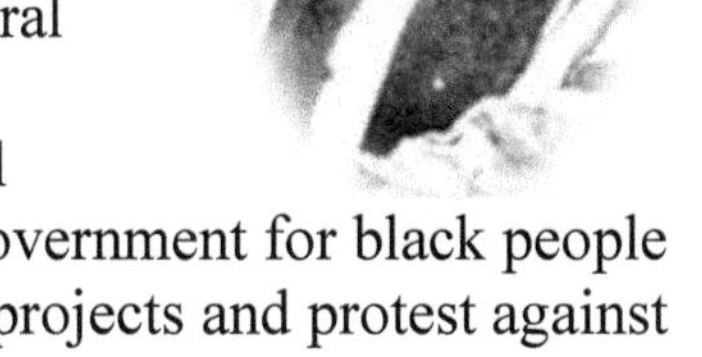

Paul Bogle (1822-1865)
A Baptist Deacon s generally regarded as a peaceful man but poverty and injustice in the society and lack of public confidence in the central authority urged Bogle to lead a protest march to the Morant Bay courthouse on 11 October 1865. He was captured and hanged on October 24, 1865 but his actions paved the way for the establishment of just practices in the courts and led to a change in official attitude which in turn enhanced the social and economic conditions of the people.

George William Gordon (1820-1865)
A self-educated landowner in St. Thomas who urged people to protest against and resist the oppressive and unjust conditions under which they were forced to live. He was arrested and charged, illegally tried by Court Martial, convicted, and executed on 23 October 1865. His death, along with that of Paul Bogle triggered the beginning of a new era in Jamaica's development - the British government became compelled to effect changes including outstanding reforms in education, health, local government, banking and infrastructure.

Samuel Sharpe (1801-1832)

"I would rather die upon yonder gallows than live in slavery". Because of his intelligence and leadership qualities, Sam Sharpe became a "daddy", or leader of the native Baptists in Montego Bay. An educated town slave, preacher and spokesman Sharpe carried on the Resistance against slavery and effected the most outstanding Slave Rebellion in Jamaica's history. The 1831 Rebellion started in St. James on December 28 and spread throughout the entire island. Sam Sharpe was eventually captured and hung at the Parade in Montego Bay (now Sam Sharpe Square). In 1834 the Abolition Bill was passed by the British Parliament and in 1838 slavery was abolished.

Nanny of the Maroons

A leader of the Maroons at the beginning of the 18th century, Nanny was regarded by both the Maroons and the British settlers as an outstanding military leader who became a symbol of unity and strength for her people during times of crisis. She possessed a fierce fighting spirit and her cleverness in planning guerrilla warfare confused the British who dreaded the Maroon traps set for them. Nanny met her untimely death sometime around 1734. Yet, the spirit of Nanny of the Maroons remains today as a symbol of that indomitable desire that will never yield to captivity.

National Anthem

The Anthem is the creative work of: The late Rev. & Hon. Hugh Sherlock, OJ, OBE; The late Hon. Robert Lightbourne, OJ; The late Mapletoft Poulle, and Mrs Poulle (now Mrs Raymond Lindo)

Eternal Father bless our land,
Guard us with Thy Mighty Hand
Keep us free from evil powers,
Be our light through countless hours.
To our Leaders Great Defender,
Grant true wisdom from above.
Justice, Truth be ours forever,
Jamaica Land we love.
Jamaica, Jamaica, Jamaica land we love.

Teach us true respect for all,
Stir response to duty's call.
Strengthen us the weak to cherish,
Give us vision lest we perish.
Knowledge send us Heavenly Father,
Grant true wisdom from above.
Justice, Truth be ours forever,
Jamaica, land we love.
Jamaica, Jamaica, Jamaica land we love.

National Song: I Pledge my Heart

I pledge my heart forever
To serve with humble pride
This shining homeland, ever
So long as earth abide.

I pledge my heart, this island
As God and faith shall live
My work, my strength, my love and
My loyalty to give.

O green isle of the Indies,
Jamaica, strong and free,
Our vows and loyal promises
O heartland, 'tis to Thee.

National Pledge

Before God and all mankind
I pledge the love and loyalty of my heart
The wisdom and courage of my mind
The strength and vigour of my body
In the service of my fellow citizens.

I promise to stand up for justice
Brotherhood and peace
To work diligently and creatively
To think generously and honestly
So that, Jamaica may, under God, increase in beauty
Fellowship and prosperity
And play her part in advancing the welfare of the whole
human race.

National Prayer

Let us give thanks for all God's goodness and the wonderful heritage into which we have entered:
Response to each petition: We give thee thanks, O God

For Jamaica, our island home, the land of our birth -
Response

For the majesty of our hills, the beauty of our valleys, and the flaming loveliness of our gardens –
Response

For the warmth and brightness of our days and the calm and peace of our countryside –
Response

For the rich heritage of our people coming for many races, and yet one in purpose, in achievement, and in destiny, and for the dignity of labour and the service given by every citizen of our land –
Response

For freedom, just laws and our democratic way of life –
Response

For the high privilege and responsibility of Independence and for bringing us to nationhood –
Response

For our parents, teachers, religious and other leaders and all those who in every walk of life are helping to prepare us for responsible citizenship, and for all those who are giving voluntary service in the public interest –

RESPONSE

For the poets, artists and thinkers and all who create in us the vision of a new and better society –
RESPONSE

For our godly heritage, the example of Jesus Christ and the sacrifices of our fathers in the faith –
RESPONSE

Shorter Pledge for Schools

Before God and all mankind
I pledge my love, my loyalty and skills, in the service of Jamaica and my fellow citizens.
I promise to work diligently and to help build a prosperous and peaceful nation.

Governors-General of Jamaica

Sir Kenneth William Blackburne
(6 Aug – 30 Nov 1962)

The Most Hon. Sir Clifford Clarence Campbell
(1 Dec 1962 – 2 Mar 1973)

Sir Herbert George Holwell Duffus
(2 Mar – 27 Jun 1973)
(acting)

The Most Hon. Sir Florizel Augustus Glasspole
(27 Jun 1973 –
31 Mar 1991)

Edward Zacca
(31 Mar –1 Aug 1991)
(acting)

The Most Hon. Sir Howard Felix Hanlan Cooke
(1 Aug 1991 – 15 Feb 2006)

The Most Hon. Prof. Sir Kenneth O. Hall
(15 Feb 2006 – 26 Feb 2009)

His Excellency the Most Hon. Sir Patrick Linton Allen
(26 Feb 2009 –present)

Jamaica's Prime Ministers

Sir Alexander Bustamante (JLP): 29 Apr 1962 to 23 Feb 1967

Sir Donald Sangster (JLP): 23 Feb to 11 Apr 1967

Hugh Shearer (JLP): 11 Apr 1967 to 2 Mar 1972

Michael Manley (PNP): 2 Mar 1972 to 1 Nov 1980 & 10 Feb 1989 to 30 Mar 1992

Edward Seaga (JLP): 1 Nov 1980 to 10 Feb1989

P. J. Patterson (PNP): 30 Mar 1992 to 30 Mar 2006

Portia Simpson-Miller (PNP): 30 Mar 2006 to 11 Sept 2007 **and from 5 January 2012 to Present**

Bruce Golding (JLP): 11 Sept 2007 to 23 October 2011

Andrew Holness (JLP) 23 October 2011 to 5 Jan 2012

Out of Many, One People

Jamaica has a dynamic culture and a diverse population representing the mosaic of ethnic groups that landed on the island's shores over the past several centuries.

Whether they be descendants of the colonists or more recent immigrants from other countries, people of all nationalities live and work in harmony in Jamaica. Afro-Jamaicans constitute over 90% with the remaining percentage shared among English, Scottish, Welsh, East Indians, Chinese, Lebanese, Syrians, Jews and others. This diversity is the essence of the island's motto "Out of Many, One People".

The Indians

Descendants of the immigrant workers have influenced the fields of farming, medicine, politics and even horse-racing. Names such as Chatani, Chulani, Tewani, Mahtani, Daswani, Vaswani and Chandiram have become synonymous with manufacturing, wholesale, retail and in-bond businesses providing employment for thousands of Jamaicans.

The Irish

There are many prominent Jamaicans of Irish heritage. These include poet Claude McKay, Chris Blackwell, founder of Island Records, one of Jamaica's foremost historians and former UWI Vice Chancellor - Sir Philip Sherlock, writer John Hearne, and successful horse trainer, Phillip Feanny, Surnames such as Burke, Collins, Mackey, Murphy and Madden, to name just a few, are quite common.

The Japanese

Although the Japanese were not early settlers in Jamaica, Japanese people now live on the island and many Japanese nationals take a musical pilgrimage to Jamaica. In recent times, they have embraced Jamaica's reggae/dancehall culture. Not only are there reggae artistes from the Land of the Rising Sun but there are also sound systems such as the famous Mighty Crown, which recently won the coveted Death Before Dishonour title the second year running. In 2002

'Junko Bashment' a young Japanese was crowned Dancehall Queen at the annual contest where talented women make strong fashion statements and display exceptional dance moves. Pushim, a singer dubbed 'Queen of Japanese Reggae', recorded her first album “Say Greeting” in Jamaica and has performed at Reggae Sumfest.

The Jews

Prominent Jewish Jamaicans who made an impact include Poet Daniel Lopez Laguna who converted biblical Psalms into poems; 19th century painter Isaac Mendes Belisario whose famed "Belisario" prints of Jamaican characters are cultural icons; Jacob and Joshua de Cordova who founded the "Gleaner" in 1833; Ward Theatre architect Rudolph Henriques; Jorge Ricardo Isaacs, author of ‘Maria’, considered the "national novel" of Columbia; Sir Neville Noel Ashenheim who served as Jamaica's first ambassador to Washington; the Hon. Ernest Altamont da Costa and Councillor Senator Hon. Eli Matalon, who served as Mayors of Kingston.

The Lebanese

The Lebanese gave the island a beauty queen - former Miss Jamaica and Miss World, Lisa Hanna-Panton is part Lebanese. Names like Hanna, Mahfood, Issa, Joseph, Ammar, Azan, Shoucair, Karam, Younis, Khouri, Fadil, Feanny, Dabdoub, Matalon and Ziadie are giants of retail, tourism, horse racing, industry and manufacturing. The most famous Jamaican with Lebanese descent is the Most Hon. Edward Seaga, former Prime Minister.

The Scottish

Perhaps the most infamous Scottish immigrant is Lewis Hutchison, better known as the Mad Master of Edinburgh Castle who was accused of killing travellers for sport. He was tried, found guilty and condemned to death by hanging in Spanish Town Square. More positive forms of Scottish influence can be found in Jamaican dance the scotch reel in Kingston's Scots Kirk Church, as well as in Jamaica's language.

The Welsh

The Welsh has shown their presence on the island through their buildings and craftsmsanhip including many of the slate roofs that covered Jamaican 18th & 19th century sugar works. There are also Welsh place names such as Bangor Ridge, Cardiff Hall, Llandilo, Llandovery and Pencarne. Jamaican surnames of Welsh background include: Bryan, Davis, Davies, Jones, Meredith, Morgan, Owens, Rhys/Reece, Williams and Vaughan.

GLOSSARY

Afi – has/have to
Agaen – again
Ah – at/it is
Ah fi – it belongs to
Ah good – Serves you right
Ahoa - Oh
Aise – ears
Alms ouse – nonsense
Anansi – spider
Anodda – another
Ar – her
Av – have
Ax – ask
Baaskit – basket
Backa – behind
Backle – bottle
Bad mout –speak ill of
Bad mine – jealous/ grudgeful
Bakansa – sharp answer
Bafan – clumsy/ awkward
Bandoolu – dishonest
Bangarang – disturbance/noise
Bankra – big basket
Barn – born
Bat – moth
Battam – bottom
Beanie – small
Befoe – before
Ben de – was/were
Berry – very
Bex – upset/angry
Bickle – food
Bickle – food
Big and so-so-so – big-bodied & lazy
Bline – blind
Brawta – extra
Breda – brother
Breshé – breadfruit
Bruk – break/broke
Bud – bird
Bun – burn
Bun – burn
Buss - burst
Bwile – boil
Bwoy – boy
Cackroach – cockroach

Carry-go bring-come – gossip
Cawna – corner
Chowziz – pants
Chuck – truck
Chupid – stupid
Cliding – cloying
Cobich – mean/ stingy
Coco – cocoa
Com yah – come here
Coodeh – look at that
Craben – craven
Crakup - laugh
Cratch – scratch
Crawny – look Awful/unwell
Crawses – problematic situation/person
Cruff – untidy/ unambitious
Cry-cry – cries easily
Cumbulo – peers
Cumfat - comfort
Cunnyman – conman
Cunue – canoe
Cuss – to quarrel
Cuss-cuss – quarrel
Cut yeye – to look at someone in disdain
Cuya – look at this
Cyaan – cannot
Dan – than
Danki – donkey
Dat – that
Dawg – dog
De - the
Deble – devil
Ded lef – inheritance
Dégé dégé – only
Deh – there/is
Deh deh – is there
De bout – around/ nearby
Dem – them
Di – the
Diay – day
Doah – door
Doan – don't
Dongkia – carefree
Doze – those
Dress back – step back/reverse

Dung – down
Duont it? – isn't that so?
Duppy – ghost
Dut – earth/soil
Dutty – dirty
Dweet – do it
Ebery – every
Ih – it
Ih-he – yes
Ef - if
Ef a so, a so – so be it
Facety – feisty/ saucy
Fah – for
Fall dung – fall
Fallaw – follow
Fala bak a mi – follow me
Fambily – family
Farrid – forehead
Fass – inquisitive
Fasser - faster
Fedda – feather
Fenké fenké – slight/weak
Fi – for/to
Fiah – fire
Firetick – fire-stick
Fiwi – ours
Flim – film
Fluxy – flaccid/ squashy
Fool-fool – silly/stupid
Foot bottam – sole of the foot
Force ripe – unnaturally mature
Frak tail – hemline
Frouzi – smelly
Fur – far
Gaah farin - go abroad
Gahlang – go on
Gastu – must
Get chruu – succeed
Ghana – gone to
Ginal – trickster/ dishonest person
Gi a six fi a nain – deceive
Goh – go
Goh dung – go down
Gonna – going to...
Gravalicious – greedy

Grung – ground/ cultivated field
Guweh – go away
Gwaan – go on
Gwine – going to
Gyal – girl
Haad – hard
Hab – has/have
Hackle – hassle/ bother
Haffi – have/has to
Halla – holler/cry out loudly
Han – hand
Han middle – palm
Hat - painful
Hea - hear
Head top – crown of the head
Hebby – heavy
Heng – hang
Henka – hanging around for food
Hitey titey – snobbish
Hush – be comforted
Ih – It
Ih-ih – no
Im – him
Inna – In /Into
Jankro – vulture/ crow
Jankro Batty – Unpurified white rum
Jing-bang – lots of useless items
Jook – pierce/poke
Jrap fut – to dance
Juck - pierce
Junjo – mould
Kak op – to raise
Keba – cover
Kekkle – kettle/ pot
Ketch – catch/ caught
Kibba - cover
Kin pupalick – to do a somersault
Kin teet – grin
Kot ten – to sit with legs crossed
Krai kree – to call time-out
Krismus – Christmas
Kuh ya – look here
Kumoochin – mean/stingy
Kuul-yu-fut – relax
Kya – care

Labba labba – gossip
Laffi-laffi – giggly
Laka se - as if
Lang – long
Langa – longer
Larn – learn
Lenky – lanky
Lib – live
Libati tekin – presumptious attitude
Libba – liver
Lick - hit
Licky licky – suck up to/greedy
Likkle – little
Lilly – little
Limba – limber
Lob – love
Lyad – liar
Ma – mother/ madam
Macca – thorn
Mada – mother
Maggige – maggot
Mannas – manners
Mash up – destroy/ break up
Maskitta – mosquito
Massa – mister
Mawga – meagre /malnourished
Meja - measure
Mek – make
Memba – remember
Mi – me
Miehke-miehke – messy/distasteful
Mikhase – hurry up
Mout – mouth
Mout-a-massy – someone who talks too much
Mucky – filthy
Mumma – mother
Munstah – monster
Mussi – must
Muss-muss – mouse
Naah – not going to
Nebber – never
Nize – noise
Noh – does not
Nowey - nowhere
Nuff – plenty/ brazen
Nutten – nothing
Nutting – nothing
Nyam – eat
Oddah – other
Ooman – woman

Outa haada – rude/ imprudent
Out fi – about to
Owna – owner
Packi - vessel made from a gourd
Pan – on
Passa passa – mix up
Patoo – owl
PawPaw – papaya
Peenywally – firefly
Peteta – potato
Pickney – young child
Picky-picky – choosey/sparse
Poah – poor
Poppyshow – laughable/show off
Pread – spread
Prekeh – one who thinks much of himself but is in fact a laughing stock
Pupa – father
Pushi – push it
Puss – cat
Putto-putto – soft
Puttus – sweetheart
Pwoil – spoil
Pyaa-pyaa – sickly/feeble
Quint – blink
Ramp – play
Red yeye – envious
Renk – foul smell/rude
Rivva – river
Roun – around
Run a boat – informal cooking
Sa – sir
Sabe – save
Saggle – saddle
Sake a – because of
Seame weigh – just like that
Sarry – sorry
Seh feh – dare me
Shaat – short
Shaata – shorter
Shedda – shadow
Sheg up – to disappoint
Shi – she
Shuub – shove/push
Si – see
Siddong – sit down

Sinting – something
Slackniss – lewd/ vulgar behaviour
Sleep up – coagulate
Smaddy – somebody
Soppm – something
Sopsy – weak/ soft/puny
Spirit tek – have an affinity with
Stranja – stranger
Stush – snobbish
Se-se – gossip
Su-su – to gossip
Swallaw – swallow
Stush – snobbish
Su-su – carry news/ gossip
Swo-so – mediocre
Tallawah – impressive
Tan – stand/stay/is
Tan deh – stay there
Tan up – stand up
Tap – Stop/top
Tea – any hot drink
Teddy – steady
Tegereg – person of no class/uncouth
Tek – take
Tenk yuh – thank you
Tick – stick
Ticker – thicker
Ticky ticky – young children/fish
Tideh – today
Ting – thing
Togeda – together
Trampooz – to walk about
Trow – throw
Trubble – trouble
Tun – turn
Uhnu – you all
Umhm – yes
Waagen? – what else?
Waah - want
Wah – what
Wallah – wallow
Warra warra – (used instead of a curseword)
Wash – sugar & Water mixed
Weh – where/away
Wha – what
Wha-ah gwaan – what's happening?

Wha mek –why
Whappen – what's up?
Wi – we
Wid – with
Wingy – small/ feeble
Wod – word
Woss – worse/ worst
Wosser – worse
Wuk – work
Wukliss – worthless
Yah - here
Yasso – here
Yeye – eye
Yout – youth
Yuh – you

www.ingramcontent.com/pod-product-compliance
Ingram Content Group UK Ltd.
Pitfield, Milton Keynes, MK11 3LW, UK
UKHW021051270726
13967UKWH00012B/466